Creature Features

Edited By Daisy Job

First published in Great Britain in 2020 by:

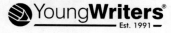

Young Writers
Remus House
Coltsfoot Drive
Peterborough
PE2 9BF
Telephone: 01733 890066
Website: www.youngwriters.co.uk

All Rights Reserved
Book Design by Ashley Janson
© Copyright Contributors 2019
Softback ISBN 978-1-83928-700-8

Printed and bound in the UK by BookPrintingUK
Website: www.bookprintinguk.com
YB0429P

FOREWORD

Hello Reader!

For our latest poetry competition we sent out funky and vibrant worksheets for primary school pupils to fill in and create their very own poem about fiendish fiends and crazy creatures. I got to read them and guess what? They were **roarsome**!

The pupils were able to read our example poems and use the fun-filled free resources to help bring their imaginations to life, and the result is pages **oozing** with exciting poetic tales. From friendly monsters to mean monsters, from bumps in the night to **rip-roaring** adventures, these pupils have excelled themselves, and now have the joy of seeing their work in print!

Here at Young Writers we love nothing more than poetry and creativity. We aim to encourage children to put pen to paper to inspire a love of the written word and explore their own unique worlds of creativity. We'd like to congratulate all of the aspiring authors that have created this book of **monstrous mayhem** and we know that these poems will be enjoyed for years to come. So, dive on in and submerge yourself in all things furry and fearsome (and perhaps check under the bed!).

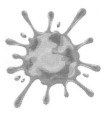

CONTENTS

Bushvalley Primary School, Stranocum

Isaac Cordner (9)	1
Summer-Rose Ann Dempster (9)	2
Allana Foster (8)	3
Billie Josephine Gretta Donaldson (9)	4
Kyra Ann Guy (10)	5
Hayley McCooke (9)	6
Mark Inglis (8)	7
Lucy Bartlett (9)	8
Reuben Zach Wilmot (9)	9
Carson McKay (8), Emily, Leon, Leah & Steven McConaghy (9)	10
Kayley Gough (8)	11
Caleb McMullan (8)	12
Miley-Rose McCooke (8)	13
Sophie Jessica Taylor (9)	14
Saul Alex Baird (10)	15
Tom McDowell (9)	16
Lucas Boreland (10)	17
Rowan Taggart (8)	18
Kristian Neil (10)	19

Cawood CE Primary School, Cawood

Seren Olivia Hughes (8)	20
Oliver Thomas Davenport (8)	21
Heather Hewick (8)	22
Enya Kate Drum (8)	23
Dulcie Buckley (8)	24
Isla Woodmason (8)	25

Even Swindon Primary School, Raybrook Park

Emily Karina Buckley-Wells (8)	26
Nazeefa Talukder (11)	28
Amelia Adrych (11)	30
Maisy Bond (9)	31
Isabelle Lola Giles (9)	32
Talia Rose Mitchell (8)	33
Paige Jessop (8)	34
Hriti Pande (10)	35
Elizabeth Rose McDanielson (8)	36
Ava Wedge (8)	37
Ojasvi Verma (11)	38
Natasza Jasinska (9)	39
Grace Crowter (10)	40
Sahaj Malik (9)	41
Anne Sim (7)	42
Mollie-Mae Birt (9)	43
Aderyn Parry (9)	44
Rita Vilaca (10)	45
Ellie-May Spelman (9)	46
Chloe Morton (8)	47
Evie Amelia Adkin (8)	48
Amara Losada Lambreth (8)	49
Lilly Smith (7)	50
Amelie Webster (8)	51
Ava Hams (8)	52
Phoebe Mae Hughes (9)	53
Jamie Paul William Burnett (8)	54

Glebelands Primary Academy, Chatteris

Jacob Neil Rolph (10)	55
Sophie Mae Roberts (10)	56
Kyle Ray Stone (10)	57
Ethan James White (10)	58
Emily Mason (11)	59
Rosie May Wheelan (10)	60
Katie Barnard (10)	61
Caitlin Rose Newman (10)	62
Summer Wright (10)	63
Tamsin Allard (11)	64
Connie Wright (11)	65
Nathan Fuller (10)	66
Les Connett (10)	67
Matthew Gio Mendoza (11)	68
Izabella Samantha Schofield (11)	69
Albert Michael Hollinshead (10)	70
Lily Bell (10)	71
Emma Robins (10)	72
Brooke Hanady Ashton (10)	73
Matilda Mason-Hughes (10)	74
Harry Robert Kenneth Kerr (10)	75
Christian Conyers (10)	76
Rebecca Jayne Miller (10)	77
Taylah Parker (10)	78
Staci Brown (10)	79
Ben Carpenter-Richmond (10)	80
Zack Eccleston (10)	81
Tia-Rose Martin (10)	82
Ellie Stringer (10)	83
Bella Weaver (10)	84
Dylan Seymour (11)	85
Ruby Grace Gardner (10)	86
Alex Allen (10)	87
Spencer Thompson (10)	88
Caitlin Lenton (10)	89
Kyle Carter (10)	90
Alise Kalva (10)	91
Caitlyn Smith (10)	92
Jessica-Leigh Sessions (11)	93

Malvern St James Girls' School, Malvern

Lacey Isobelle Klima (10)	94
Isla Wall (10)	97
Izzy Lewis (11)	98
Tilly Coughtrie (9)	101
Emily Lymer (10)	102
Grace Price (9)	105
Holly Forsyth (9)	106
Emily Aris (10)	107
Jasmine Garner (9)	108
Sophia Mepsted (10)	109
Fenella Mason (11)	110
Charlotte Lorraine Gannon (11)	111
Eleanor Jayne Bradford (9)	112
Farah Aftab (9)	113
Saba Saghir (9)	114
Lauren Iris Jolley (9)	115
Sophia Michael (10)	116
Carlota de Palacio (9)	117
Beulah Naami Emmanuel (10)	118
Tilly Delamore (10)	119
Alice Kay-Jones (10)	120

Riccall Community Primary School, Riccall

Sam Anderson (10)	121
Jemma Johnson (10)	122
Nicola Louise Rodwell (11)	124
Harry Blake (10)	125
Ellie Chambers (10)	126
Oscar Squires (10)	127
Finley Woodroffe (10)	128
Sophia Astrid Robinson (10)	129
Toby Alexander Steward (10)	130
Jack Duffy (10)	131
Charlie Anderson (10)	132
Lewis Porteous (10)	133
Kadie Olivia Kettlewell (10)	134
Ashton Clayton (10)	135
Katie Rose Hardwick (10)	136
Billy Hitrof Swan (11)	137

Cameron Roche (10)	138
Laura-Rose Arkless McKie (11)	139
Ruby Baron (10)	140
Sam Quormby Gowland (10)	141
Abigail Ayre (10)	142
Millie Bradley (10)	143
Dziugas Gelbuda (11)	144
Max Butterfield (10)	145
Jake Wilman (10)	146
Georgia Saunders (10)	147
Madison Main (11)	148
Josh Light (11)	149
Oliver Capewell (11)	150
Roma Sofia Gatenby (10)	151
Luke Sparham (10)	152

St Benet's RC Primary School, Sunderland

Emily Grace Soulsby (8)	153
Emily Maw (8)	154
Scarlett Shickle (8)	155
Ella Clasper (8)	156
Damaris Osigwelem (9)	157
Evie Selkirk (8)	158
Scarlett Dawn Glendenning (8)	159
Eva Wilkinson (8)	160
Izzy Rose Balcombe (8)	161
Katie Ward (8)	162
Poppy Robson (8)	163
Hannah Elizabeth Banks (8) & Emilia Szewczyk	164
Ruby Laidler-Gilchrist (8)	165
Archie McGuire (8)	166
Daniel Hewitt (9)	167
Maddie Harrison (8)	168
Alice Wright (8)	169
Peter Rogers (8)	170
Aiesha Potts (9)	171
Isaac Fowler (8)	172
Gabriel Cleugh (9)	173

Wheatfield Primary School, Winnersh

Logan Star Henderson-Thompson (9)	174
Herbert Whitaker (9)	176
Lily Scarlett Wears (9)	177
Constance Ann Thrift (9)	178
Ava Rae Henderson-Thompson (9)	179
Evangeline Cozens (10)	180
Michael Nash (9)	181
Kai Driscoll (9)	182
Aum Patel (9)	183
Tailor Cauldwell (9)	184
Konstantinos Alkinoos Servos (9)	185
Alex Cazacu (9)	186
Ava Quinn (9)	187
Akhilesh Molala (9)	188
Vinnie Valentine (9)	189
Tiaana Amileah Lee (10)	190
Abhiram Anumolu (9)	191

THE POEMS

Petrifying Pete!

I heard about this boy who lived on my street
He lived in a cottage and his name was Pete.

But it was all rotten on his thatched roof,
The cat that they had fell off the windowsill, *poof!*

One cold, damp night
There was a growling sound that gave me a fright.

I was lying in my bed, shocked
Worried that the door wasn't locked.

Just then, the window smashed and a giant paw came through
In a growly voice, it said, "I'm coming for you!"

I ran out of the house, out on the street
Beware! Beware of the petrifying Pete!

Isaac Cordner (9)
Bushvalley Primary School, Stranocum

Once I Saw A Monster

Once I saw a monster
All big and bright.
I said, "What's wrong?"
He said, "You gave me a fright."
He had blue hair and goo on his cheek
And he had a nose like a bird's beak.
His toes were weird and crooked
So I had a look.
He said, "What are you looking at?"
I said, "You!" but he said, "Boo!"
So I ran down the stairs
To get my dad.
He wasn't there and I was sad.
I ran back up to have another look.
It turns out, the monster was my dad!
I was shook.

Summer-Rose Ann Dempster (9)
Bushvalley Primary School, Stranocum

I Think I Hear A Monster

I think I hear a monster shouting with fear
Of how to find his food over here
But where is he going
Is he coming for me?

I think I hear a monster coming over here
Shouting for his food
Crying with a sore stomach
Waiting for his food

I think I hear a monster coming closer
To me
Thinking he will find something
Wanting food to drop out of the sky

I think I hear a monster snoring away
Now I can get some sleep
But I hear something
It is silence.

Allana Foster (8)
Bushvalley Primary School, Stranocum

Ashpie

It makes a clicking sound, almost like a clock
All through the night, it looks for helpless victims
To rip to shreds
Eating your organs
Having fun
A brutal fight at midnight
Don't make a peep or it'll bite
Five days a week it comes
Killing ten to fifteen people
Don't be one today
Chit-chat all day depending on what you'll say
Might kill you tonight
Sleeping is not safe on weekdays
But on weekends, it rests peacefully
Don't wake it up.

Billie Josephine Gretta Donaldson (9)
Bushvalley Primary School, Stranocum

He's Changing

There's a funny, kind monster
Living in my closet
At night, he gives me ice cream
Playing outside in the park
Having a fun time
But when it rains, he's gone, I start to weep
He stares at you in the eye
He takes kids and eats them
And I might be next
I am creeping down the stairs and he is there
I run up and tell my mum and dad
But they are fast asleep
He's right in front of the bed
Dad gets up to turn on the light
He's gone...

Kyra Ann Guy (10)
Bushvalley Primary School, Stranocum

I Hear A Monster

I hear a monster under my bed
Is it blue? Is it green?
Does it have red eyes?
It is coming to get me
It is shouting and screaming at me
Now, run!

I hear a big monster in my house
I am scared, "Argh!"
Now, run! Go!
It is coming up my bedpost! Argh!

I run outside
The monster is there
Run, run, the monster is big
And green with red eyes
It sounds like a moaning goat of a thing
Run!

Hayley McCooke (9)
Bushvalley Primary School, Stranocum

The Best Monster Ever

I saw someone in my class
He was slimy
He's my friend
Some people run away from him
They think he's scary
But he's a good friend

I've been to his house twice
It's cool
And he lives at 24 Main Street Ballymoney
He likes to eat apple burgers

He's been to my house once
And he likes my house as well
He thinks I'm cool

My friend is a good slimy friend.

Mark Inglis (8)
Bushvalley Primary School, Stranocum

Under My Bed

I hear a monster
Eating under my bed
He is grey and white, soft and funny
He is so nice to me
But sometimes not

It is always after midnight
Somewhere beyond the shadows
There is a new monster
It is so soft
And it was eating a McDonald's
I don't know why she likes to eat McDonald's
She is nice

I see my old monster
He is so old
He is grey with blue eyes.

Lucy Bartlett (9)
Bushvalley Primary School, Stranocum

The Night Watcher

Skinny, tall and as cold as ice cubes
Dry cracks running down his face
He whooshes through the streets
Making children scream
His eyes are glowing in the dark
He likes to hide in dark spaces
To parents, he is a myth
But to kids, he's otherwise
He runs through the streets
And he grabs the kids
And he puts them in his sack
Then he says, "Mine!"

Reuben Zach Wilmot (9)
Bushvalley Primary School, Stranocum

Monster

Hairy, scary, tall and merry
Big, shark-like teeth
Smells like a pig
Can do a jig
As fast as a cheetah
His name is Rita
He eats children
And drinks their blood
Eyes red and yellow
They glow in the dark
Roars like a grizzly bear
Crawls through the night
To give you a fright.

Carson McKay (8), Emily, Leon, Leah & Steven McConaghy (9)
Bushvalley Primary School, Stranocum

I Hear A Monster

I hear a monster under my bed
Is it black or is it pink?
Does it have big eyes or small eyes?
Is it big or is it small?
Now it is staring at me in the haunted house at midnight
He was eating a Chinese on my roof
When I went into the garden
Then he saw me and ran after me
Oh no! Run, run, run!

Kayley Gough (8)
Bushvalley Primary School, Stranocum

The Little Black Bat

Fly, fly little bat
Don't be scared of the rat

If you're going now
You can go, but go quickly
And say goodbye
Will you fly?

Fly, fly little bat
That's the one I saw last night

He was black and white
Like the night
With stripes
He was a fright.

Caleb McMullan (8)
Bushvalley Primary School, Stranocum

Blue Briana

I hope I see a monster in my yard
She'd have four legs
I hope I see a monster under my bed
She'd be red, yellow and orange
I hope I see a monster
She'd have a black mouth
I hope she's not made out of gunpowder
Or she'll blow up the house
Is she real? No one knows.

Miley-Rose McCooke (8)
Bushvalley Primary School, Stranocum

My Monster

Little, tiny and sweet
Smells like roses
All pretty and neat
As wise as an owl
Quiet as a mouse
As fast as lightning
She is not very frightening
Eats chocolate marshmallows
Drinks strawberry milkshakes
Her eyes a bright blue
She likes me and you.

Sophie Jessica Taylor (9)
Bushvalley Primary School, Stranocum

The Midnight Hunter Met His Darkest Enemy

His eyes are red and fat
He sounds like a digger
He smells like doughnuts and honey
He feels slimy, sticky and hard
Blood drips down his face

He met his darkest enemy
They started to fight in a chilly graveyard
He won the fight and put him in a coffin.

Saul Alex Baird (10)
Bushvalley Primary School, Stranocum

My Monster

I saw a monster under my bed
He had black teeth
And a hairy tummy
I thought he was under my chair
He was very noisy
Thump! Thump! he went
At night-time, he crawled up my bed
Then in the day
He ran away
Into the woods with a whoosh!

Tom McDowell (9)
Bushvalley Primary School, Stranocum

The Midnight Seeker

S he stares through your window
"E erie," they all say
"E ek!" screamed one and she was never seen again
K ills the ones that talk
E volves into a nightmare
"R oar!" and you're gone.

Lucas Boreland (10)
Bushvalley Primary School, Stranocum

The Creaking Door

The door was creaking open
A hairy monster came in
The little boy was very frightened
A monster was roaring,
"Come here, little boy.
Teatime, little boy.
I'm waiting, little boy.
I have food..."

Rowan Taggart (8)
Bushvalley Primary School, Stranocum

The Thing

Tall, slow and fat
He's quite a fright
He flies through the night
Without any light
He's quite light
To make it easy
To fly through the dark, black night.

Kristian Neil (10)
Bushvalley Primary School, Stranocum

What's That In The Grass?

What's in the grass? Is it a four-headed snake?
Wow! Amazing! What is it called?
The Four-Headed Titanaboa, watch out!
Titanaboa is big and spiky, don't touch it

Though it's friendly, let's go play
How amazing, it runs at everyone and gets stuck in the mud
Amazing chaser he is
Though he's really feisty

In the grass, he's really fast
No way, look at it now!

Grass, that's where we should look
And round up that lizard
And look! I found it!
So amazing!

Seren Olivia Hughes (8)
Cawood CE Primary School, Cawood

Kevin

Kevin is my monster, we share everything
When he visits me in the night
I cry out in delight.
We play together in the dark
We have to be quiet
We don't want to wake my brother, Mark
Last Sunday, we had a fun day in the park.
We played until it got dark
Kevin's funny, Kevin's kind
And he also has a clever mind
I hope my teachers never find
All the homework he's done this time.
When I grow up, I hope he never goes away
Because then I'll see him every day.

Oliver Thomas Davenport (8)
Cawood CE Primary School, Cawood

My Monster Sloppy

Some of my monsters are ever so tall
Some of my monsters are ever so small
But Sloppy is the best monster of all

Sloppy always shouts out, "Yay!"
When girls and boys come to play
Sloppy eats the crumbs off the floor
And always seems to want some more
Sloppy says he's always hungry
But he has never eaten anybody

The reason Sloppy's my best friend
Is because he will love me to the end.

Heather Hewick (8)
Cawood CE Primary School, Cawood

Deloper The Three-Eyed Monster

Deloper the shape-shifter is no sloper
With fluffy hands and sticky pads
Eyes like horns and enormous fangs
Beware he doesn't catch you with his four giant hands
He casts a long shadow that will fill you with fright
He's as fast as a fox, so run for your life
Bang! Bang! Bang! as he thunders along
The three-eyed monster, here I come!

Enya Kate Drum (8)
Cawood CE Primary School, Cawood

Yogol, Boomer And Dotty

No monster is better than Yogol
Because he has no head
His friend is Boomer
With no head or bed
Boomer's friend is Dotty
With no bed, head or legs
No monster is better than Dotty
Because she has no legs
Everyone cheer for Dotty
Because she is spotty.

Dulcie Buckley (8)
Cawood CE Primary School, Cawood

Slime

His name is Slime
He's full of green and grime
When he's in my room
I feel like it's my doom
And, all the shivers inside of me
I feel like I might pee.

Isla Woodmason (8)
Cawood CE Primary School, Cawood

The Curse Monster

He haunts the streets at night
Transformer by the day so bright
One minute in the shape of a busy bee
The next, he'll curse me
Along the corridor, up the stairs
Oh no! He's lurking there!
A street lamp would flicker as his powers unleash
His curse a spirit to rest inside us all
Upsetting us until the day we all fall
Untransformed, he wasn't normal at all
But then, when was he?
Fur covered in disgusting green slime
Feet concealed with dusty, grey grime
Other monsters would call it sublime
A fur yellow coat
And a nose like an upturned boat
Great horns sat upon his head
Above two pools of deep, deep red
A world, a one too sore
And the houses, you'll never knock on those doors
A shiny, red apple like never before

But rotten, grey pulp inside
There's nowhere to hide
Only one girl had enough courage to pluck up
When everybody else got stuck
To travel into the wood
But there, a furious monster stood
"Argh! Argh! Argh!"

Emily Karina Buckley-Wells (8)
Even Swindon Primary School, Raybrook Park

The Creature

It has been there for a while
The creature underneath my bed
I hope it doesn't bite
Because when I switch off the light
My room is as dark as night

But when I tell my parents
It doesn't go quite right
My father says I'm dreaming
And my mother shakes her head
But I guess they don't believe in
The creature underneath my bed

So that night, I wake up
Hearing growls underneath my bed
But sadly, it doesn't leave until it is very well fed
The rustling under his breath
Makes sharp shivers up my spine

It smells like putrid meat
That scrunches up my tummy
It seems to like my blood

And that makes me want to trick him
A big gulp down my throat
Means I'm his next victim...

Nazeefa Talukder (11)
Even Swindon Primary School, Raybrook Park

There's One Behind You!

Fangs are monsters no one knew about
They will act like fluffy, cute, rosy teddies
But at night, it scares your doom
Whoosh! It goes behind you, you really didn't see?
Oh well, it's over sweetie, it's just like Halloween

Fangs are monsters with big, scary teeth
I hope Santa doesn't see this
It would scare the elves away
No presents to be found underneath the Christmas tree
Only one fluffy, pink ball
Bang! It crashed upon the fireplace
You didn't see again?
Well, tough luck again
I hope to not see him again
You'd better believe me now
There's one on your back
You'd better shove it off before it goes too far!

Amelia Adrych (11)
Even Swindon Primary School, Raybrook Park

Dribbler

D ribbler is ugly and dribbles everywhere
R ude monsters call him names but he doesn't sit down and cry
I nstead, he stands up to bullies and walks on by
B ullies are the ones that have the ugliness inside
B rave Dribbler sits back and ignores them and stands up for his friends
L oving Dribbler is not mean and horrible, he is very kind-hearted
E verybody is different, not everyone is the same, it doesn't matter what you look like on the outside, it's what you're like on the inside
R emember to be like Dribbler: brave, loving and kind. Don't be like bullies that have no friends and are left behind.

Maisy Bond (9)
Even Swindon Primary School, Raybrook Park

The Friendly Monster!

What's that crick crack under my bed?
Am I really hearing this or is it in my head?
What is that shadow on the door
And the vibrating on the floor?
Its foot was sticking out so I could see it
So I peeked under the bed and what appeared to me
Was that the foot was a paw
What I thought was drool was puddles of helpless tears
I looked towards the monster and thought
Should I run? Should I scream?
Should I help it or let it be free?
Then he smiled at me and hugged me tight
And I did the same back
It seemed to me that he needed a friend
And I think that was me.

Isabelle Lola Giles (9)
Even Swindon Primary School, Raybrook Park

The Gymnasium Monster

Gym the gymnasium monster was a collector
He liked to use his metal detector
When he heard a buzz, he got all in a fuzz
He hid in the dark cupboard until the gymnasts arrived
Then he'd have the pick of their treasures
For his own pleasures
Gym would collect the things he liked most
While trying to be as quiet as a ghost
He liked the guards, the chalk and the loops
But most of all, he loved to steal the gymnastics hula hoops
After all the gymnasts went home
The naughty monster came out and did gymnastics
When the gymnasts went home
The monster didn't like being alone.

Talia Rose Mitchell (8)
Even Swindon Primary School, Raybrook Park

Monster Slime

Monster slime on my bed, all over the kitchen
Monster slime, monster slime, there is more
Let's find more over the house
Where could it be? Let's see
Is it in the kitchen? Is it in the bathroom?
Oh, that's a mushroom
No way, why is it there as well?
A pear and a big, furry bear over there
What is that? It's a big, slimy monster
Argh! Oh no! Where has it gone?
There was none of the slimy slime anymore
Now there's more and more
I think I found it, where? Over there on the stair.

Paige Jessop (8)
Even Swindon Primary School, Raybrook Park

Stories In The Dark

Stories in the deep
Stories in the dark
Stories about horrible monsters
But, under the water
There's a terrible monster
You don't know, but you still fear
She slithers in the ocean depths
Beyond human reach
Her jaws are as long as your body
Her body is much longer than yours
Her eyes are like burning pools of fire
Her scales are tougher than wire
She is a nightmare to all the living
She's the monster of the dark
Stay away or you're in trouble!

Hriti Pande (10)
Even Swindon Primary School, Raybrook Park

The Anti-Bully Monster

S he can turn into teachers and tell bullies off
T his friendly creature may look fiendish, but is very kind
E ven if you just bully one person, it will turn into the person you bully
P laying with you when you'd like a new friend
H elpful, furry and shape-shifting monster, but as they say, never judge a book by its cover
A sking bullies, "How would you feel if this happened to you?"
N ever be friends with a bully.

Elizabeth Rose McDanielson (8)
Even Swindon Primary School, Raybrook Park

Meatava

M eatava only comes out with the moon
O n Halloween, coming soon
N aughty and nice, she also breathes ice
S hort and spotty, she loves to eat mice
T roublemaker flies high and breaks everything in her path
E ating and gulping with her long tongue, there's only one thing in the world she wouldn't dare eat: her best friend Marth
R olling and running, flying and jumping, this monster is always active.

Ava Wedge (8)
Even Swindon Primary School, Raybrook Park

Choco In My House

She sneaks in the dark
As the dogs bark
She breaks your house window
The only thing you can see is her shadow

When the moon turns up
The chocolate is gulped
When it's time for sunrise
She runs away and hides

Her monstrous growls can be heard under the bed
She peeps with her eye, which is red
Her blue eyes keep a watch, all three
I can feel the scariness bubbling in me.

Ojasvi Verma (11)
Even Swindon Primary School, Raybrook Park

The Last Play Of October

Above the mountains and in the clouds
Sits an evil beast
From far away, you can hear the sounds
Of her preparing the feast
She's as red as a demon
Evil like a gnat
When it's the last day of October
Nessa will make you go splat
On the table, there lies brains, maggots and dead cats
When you look through the peephole of your bedroom door
Vanessa will turn you into a bat!

Natasza Jasinska (9)
Even Swindon Primary School, Raybrook Park

The Krackodon

He roams through the sea
Waiting for you to come into the sea
Make sure you don't look at him
Otherwise, you'll end up hypnotised
He has the sharpest claws
Hunting for you
He likes to eat fish and flesh of humans
To him, they're the perfect treat
So stay away from him and the beaches
Make sure you don't see him
'Cause he's ready for you!

Grace Crowter (10)
Even Swindon Primary School, Raybrook Park

Peckish And Brave Monster

Amongst the forest
After the swirling wind
Had found its way home
I made up my mind to have a picnic
Near the loch alone
As I ate my sandwich
I saw a creature looking like a witch
As I turned my head up
I made a noise like a gulp
The monstrous eyes were staring, all three
The scariness was crawling into me
Mr Brave Monster was there!
Run! Run!

Sahaj Malik (9)
Even Swindon Primary School, Raybrook Park

What You Have To Look Like To Be A Stretch Monster

Monster, monster, slimy and small
Monster, monster is only tall
Slimy, sticky and also sleek
You could float down a river creek
Monster, monster, two metres wide
You could swim under the sea's tide
Monster, monster is like a loyal pet
You could take monsters to the monster vet
With six eyes
They're like three spies.

Anne Sim (7)
Even Swindon Primary School, Raybrook Park

Beware Of Tickles!

Beware of Tickles, he is mighty and dangerous
He has a big smile that is very contagious
He tickles a lot from time to time
He loves maths on a number line
He likes humming
While the bees are buzzing
His favourite colour is white
And he does everything right
And I remember all the time
That this big cutie is all mine!

Mollie-Mae Birt (9)
Even Swindon Primary School, Raybrook Park

Great Big Blue Monster

As he stomps around town
He makes a faint frown
He can bound down streets
He can bound over peaks
But no one can catch him

All day
All night
When it isn't bright
His light
No longer shines

When he smiles
Everyone ends up in piles
But now he tumbles to the ground
Now he has been found.

Aderyn Parry (9)
Even Swindon Primary School, Raybrook Park

Little Devil!

I hear a little laugh
It is the little devil
Out to make some mayhem
It makes a loud crash!

It falls on you
Little Miss Devil
Will walk all over town
Until it's all mayhem

When you hear her little giggle
Like, "Hehe!"
You'd better run
Or bad luck comes your way!

Rita Vilaca (10)
Even Swindon Primary School, Raybrook Park

The Monster Called Snugglebugs

My monster is called Snugglebugs
She likes to live in the forest
She goes into the forest every day
She sneezes and sneezes just like me
Snugglebugs loves cuddles and kisses
Also boys, cute boys
She loves Tiana and cats just like me
And my friends, like my teacher
Everyone is so cute like me!

Ellie-May Spelman (9)
Even Swindon Primary School, Raybrook Park

Goomer

My mum is always telling me
There are no monsters creeping over me
But the only thing she didn't see
Was the invisible monster Goomer

Even though he's invisible and creepy
I heard, if you laugh so loud
He loses all his power.

Chloe Morton (8)
Even Swindon Primary School, Raybrook Park

Big Mouth Tutu's Adventure

M onsters are fake, they are not real
O n and off eating
N one of them are alive
S tart to search, they are everywhere
T orture, they are
E verybody hates them
R un, they are coming.

Evie Amelia Adkin (8)
Even Swindon Primary School, Raybrook Park

Scary Dreary Little Fairy

Scary Dreary Little Fairy
Why are you so small and hairy?
Hairy Fairy, why are you so small and scary?
Scary Fairy likes to play hide-and-seek every day
Scary Fairy likes pink but she always gets covered in ink.

Amara Losada Lambreth (8)
Even Swindon Primary School, Raybrook Park

Monsters On Halloween

Monsters on Halloween will not share
Monsters on Halloween will not care
Monsters on Halloween will be scary like a bear
Monsters on Halloween will make dirty air
Monsters on Halloween will never make it fair.

Lilly Smith (7)
Even Swindon Primary School, Raybrook Park

Monster

M anny the monster
O f the sea
N ever seen a monster
S carier than he
T errifying boys
E verywhere he goes
R emember to look and listen for noise.

Amelie Webster (8)
Even Swindon Primary School, Raybrook Park

Ned

N ever take anything from Ned the crazy monster
E veryone is food to scary Ned and he always eats four humans a day
D ay by day, Ned gets tired and starts to sleep all winter long.

Ava Hams (8)
Even Swindon Primary School, Raybrook Park

Gross Slime

His gross slime is divine
At night, his eyes shine
He even knows how to rhyme
He only goes at night-time
He's the best mime
He's the same colour as a lime.

Phoebe Mae Hughes (9)
Even Swindon Primary School, Raybrook Park

The Monsters I Know

The monsters I know are friendly
Monsters can make a bridge
Monsters are great
Monsters stick up for each other
Monsters eat dinner in one gulp.

Jamie Paul William Burnett (8)
Even Swindon Primary School, Raybrook Park

The Dream Destroyer

N ight comes around, you will hear no sound
I s it under your bed? No, it must be in your head
G o and have a peep, it must not want you to eat
H is magical powers put you to sleep, you won't even be able to leap
T he powers of sleep will make you weep, because of that, he will always be seen
M any sharp teeth will be used, you may be abused
A re you ready to be scared or are you ready to be prepared?
R eady to see your demise, he can see it through his red eyes
E very child is scared, they are not prepared for what is about to happen to them.

Jacob Neil Rolph (10)
Glebelands Primary Academy, Chatteris

The Sleepy Teacher-Eater

This drooling thing lurks at night
To give your teachers a scary fright
The greedy children it doesn't eat
So kids do not freak if you meet

In the day, it doesn't appear
But during the night, your teachers disappear
In the day, where does it go?
That's only for the teachers to know

From house to house, it will go
Things in its way, it will throw
Little things it will leave
That the kids that find could keep

It has unique wings to fly away
And poisonous drool to save the day
Teachers, beware
You might breathe your last piece of air.

Sophie Mae Roberts (10)
Glebelands Primary Academy, Chatteris

Creature Teacher

C rawling, creeping, sneaking around
R eady for her dinner
E very day, she waits for them
A ll the children are in danger
"T oo easy!" she would say
U gly to the core
R emember, she is very fiery
E than, Erol and Jimmy next

T ime for lunch
"E vie!" she will call
"A rgh!" everyone would scream
"C ome here!" she would beckon
"H elp!"
E rol, Ethan and Jimmy are gone
R avenous teacher.

Kyle Ray Stone (10)
Glebelands Primary Academy, Chatteris

Night Crawler

In the middle of the night
Comes a fright
To haunt your bedroom every night
Spiky teeth, pointy horns may act like a saw
Bouncing from house to house
Pouncing on people with his mouth

Being chased by every cop
He just gives them a big wallop
Faster than any car
Also he can run really far
Eating you up
In one piece
Gives him his favourite meal to eat
Mr Spook can go to you
Just to have a meal and look

Don't sleep every night
Or you'll get a fright
So be careful for your life.

Ethan James White (10)
Glebelands Primary Academy, Chatteris

Fluffy Fingerling

Fluffy little Fingerling
Isn't it so cute?

Hops onto your bed at night
Its size is so acute

It slowly licks your finger
Without giving you a fright

It does this to allow lovely dreams
And a happy goodnight

It picks out the best dreams for you
For it is on your side

It will help you through your childhood
Until you've moved on and thrown it aside

So treasure your fluffy Fingerling until you're grey and old
If not, you may have made your dreams dark and cold.

Emily Mason (11)
Glebelands Primary Academy, Chatteris

Demon Mastermind

In the depths of the creepiest forest
Dark and smelling foul
A weird sound meets the ear
A horrifying growl

A trail of bright green, glowing slime
Is leading to the streets
The young children have no idea
What a terrifying treat

He slithers across to a battered house
And hauls open the door
As quiet as a baby mouse
He tries not to make a roar

Suddenly he turns around
And makes his fingers snap
He takes flight and disappears
With a deafening crack!

Rosie May Wheelan (10)
Glebelands Primary Academy, Chatteris

Monstrous Beasts

Hiding under your bed
Living in your dreams
Waiting to scare you out of your skin
Leaving echoes of screams

Their turquoise and lilac fur covers the skin
Teeth like spears show the power within
Horns and tail hide the scars from fights
Tentacles wrap around him

Hoping to catch a two-legged foe
Giving a scare to humans here and there
This monstrous creature hides in the shadows
This devilish monster scares children everywhere.

Katie Barnard (10)
Glebelands Primary Academy, Chatteris

The Lie Detector Monster

When you lie, he will find
The truth you'd really like to hide
For when you lie, he will appear
And whisper this in your ear

You really need to find the truth
You need to do it to save your youth
But, if you lie again
On that same night, he will come back in

He uses his power to turn you old
Tell the truth and you'll be bold
And back to your young self you will go
All you had to do was

Tell the truth!

Caitlin Rose Newman (10)
Glebelands Primary Academy, Chatteris

The Monster And The Seed

In the shadows of a street
Lay a monster ready to eat

He's a sneaky monster
Ready to do its deed
He looked on the concrete ground
And saw a seed

He didn't know what to do
So he put it in his shoe

All of a sudden, he started to float
In a flash, he saw a coat

He wanted to get down
But then everything turned brown

He fell down from the sky
And never wanted to fly again.

Summer Wright (10)
Glebelands Primary Academy, Chatteris

The Very Scary Creature!

I hear a monstrous growl under my bed
But all I can see is a very green head
I can smell the bubbling slime
And I see one big eye
What could it be
With its very big eye?

I pretend to sleep and I feel some fur
I open my eyes to a big surprise
A giant creature over me with light green fur

But the only things that scare me
Are his very big eyes
I won't sleep now for the entire night!

Tamsin Allard (11)
Glebelands Primary Academy, Chatteris

Child Sucker

Bone-crusher
Blood-sucker
Flesh-muncher
Ear-twister

Creeping into the light
Giving you a huge fright
Sucking children up a pipe
Testing if they are ripe

But beware
If you have too much hair
You'll be spat back into the air
3D you'll not be
As thin as paper like Flat Stanley

If at night, you hear a "Shh!"
Shout out in case he is about.

Connie Wright (11)
Glebelands Primary Academy, Chatteris

The Demonic Demon Dog

A creature of red and black
When you wonder where your teacher is
And when you enter her room, you see
Claw marks everywhere

When a solar eclipse comes
A demon dog travels through different dimensions
Like a savage dog, it attacks everything
It isn't like the others that have one head and tail
But this one has two heads and two tails
Some people call it the Demon Dog of Death.

Nathan Fuller (10)
Glebelands Primary Academy, Chatteris

Never Say 'Fear'

In a dark, gloomy night
Lives a beast to give you a fright
Call the police, you might
Die without a fight!

In a swish and swoosh
A crack and slash
Lots of blood
Is where the monster forms

It has many different names like the Fear Feeder
He always escapes from the police
To a point where he's almost unsusceptible
Just promise to never say, "Fear."

Les Connett (10)
Glebelands Primary Academy, Chatteris

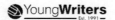

The Razor-Worm

In a mythical forest in the darkest of nights,
There is only one monster that will give you a fright,
A slimy beast that wiggles and squirms,
It is called the Razor-Worm.
With a big name for a species so small,
Its destiny is to wreck buildings so big and so tall,
While breaking houses and breaking walls,
It ruins the planet until it collapses, dies and falls.

Matthew Gio Mendoza (11)
Glebelands Primary Academy, Chatteris

Great George The Soul-Eater

Slowly, he haunts the house
Walking around and around
There stands Great George
Haunting the house day by day
Month by month
Year by year
He is a childish soul-eater
Who lies in the walls
Until night falls
No one can see him
Not even a fly
Not even a mouse
One day, a child lay down
Then was gone
Where is the child?

Izabella Samantha Schofield (11)
Glebelands Primary Academy, Chatteris

Godzilla

A gigantic creature
With a roar that you can make
He's got tiny eyes
And lights up the skies
But he's bigger than the Empire State

This beast is amazingly scary
If there's a safe place, you shouldn't be late
But, to your surprise
You'll go to the skies
And next time, don't use yourself as bait.

Albert Michael Hollinshead (10)
Glebelands Primary Academy, Chatteris

The Teacher Monster

T he teacher monster would kill in one second
E at you up and you'll be dead
A monster you think is scary but this one is more than that
C ry your eyes out but I won't care
H ave some time before you die
E ven though you're small and cute, you will be gone in a toot
R eady to die.

Lily Bell (10)
Glebelands Primary Academy, Chatteris

The Cupcake-Eater

Cupcake has a snotty nose
And when she is scared
She hides under the bed
She eats like she has not eaten in ages
And she has spots all over her face
When people walk by
She becomes scared

Her feet are sore each day
And she is joyful and she eats chocolate
And she has a smiley mouth.

Emma Robins (10)
Glebelands Primary Academy, Chatteris

Don't Let The Bed Bugs Bite

A hairy beast is what he is
A snotty human-gobbler he can't resist
His really long tongue to lick your face
He'll come really close
He won't be afraid
Be careful when you're in bed
He'll be ready
So just watch out
Snuke will be there
Stay really steady...

Brooke Hanady Ashton (10)
Glebelands Primary Academy, Chatteris

The Nightmare

In the silent alleyway of London
There sits a flesh-eating
Bone-grinding monster

Beware of night
After night, children disappear
For they have been given a fright

So, hide under the covers
For all you know
His beady eyes could be looking at you
Right now!

Matilda Mason-Hughes (10)
Glebelands Primary Academy, Chatteris

Night, Night

In the night
You may have a fright
You look around
For the sound
But nothing can be found
You hear once more
A fearful roar
You jump up quick
And find a stick
Trembling with fear
The noise is near
All at once
You are attacked
The monster is back.

Harry Robert Kenneth Kerr (10)
Glebelands Primary Academy, Chatteris

One-Eyed, One-Horned, Flying, Purple People-Eater

When you spot him
Duck away
He'll eat you in a scoff
Make sure he doesn't see you
He will eat your bones
Eat your flesh
He'll eat you in a flash
He hides in trees, in your house
He'll surprise you so you have a fright
In a flash, you'll be gone.

Christian Conyers (10)
Glebelands Primary Academy, Chatteris

The Noise-Maker

Noise-Maker
Snot-trickler
Flesh-eater

You go upstairs
You will hear him
The Noise-Maker
If you leave it
You'll never see it again
In your life
But, if you hear it
It's not gone
Good luck
Slobby, slimy
Slithering on the floor.

Rebecca Jayne Miller (10)
Glebelands Primary Academy, Chatteris

The Manners Monster

Manners, bandanas, they all seem to rhyme
But when it comes to the Manners Monster
Nothing seems to rhyme
You start to sneeze, burp and hiccup
Until you forget
Then the monster will walk out
As happy as can be
Squelching and squealing
Laughing more than a bee.

Taylah Parker (10)
Glebelands Primary Academy, Chatteris

The One-Eyed Monster

M outh that is slimy
O ne beady eye to watch things
N ose that has a good sense of smell
S tinky body
T eeth that are sharp enough to chew humans
E vil monster
R ed, bright nose that glistens in the night.

Staci Brown (10)
Glebelands Primary Academy, Chatteris

The Nightmare Dreanoty

D ead as he seems
R ead as much as you deem
E ven though you know so much
A lthough he's too tough
N o place to run or hide
O r to dive
T o have neither of these
Y ou will cease to exist.

Ben Carpenter-Richmond (10)
Glebelands Primary Academy, Chatteris

A Monster

A monster from the depths
The colour of a bull
As you get closer
You can see the body

Get too close and you could be dinner
Be quiet and silent
Let him go by, for all you know
He could be out of sight.

Zack Eccleston (10)
Glebelands Primary Academy, Chatteris

Sully

Sully
Big, blue, ruffled hair
Charging, brandishing, scaring
The greatest scarer, nightmare-maker
Rampaging, thundering, creeping
Devil horns, small, green blob
Mike.

Tia-Rose Martin (10)
Glebelands Primary Academy, Chatteris

The Grinch And The Vampire

Grinch
Christmas-stealer, bright green
Sprinting, leaping, sliding
Takes the presents, sucks your blood
Flying, murdering, scaring
Black clothes, white face
Vampire.

Ellie Stringer (10)
Glebelands Primary Academy, Chatteris

Monster Poem

Venom-spitter
Dream-shredder
Mirror-cracking
Dreaded bite

Ten thousand eyes
Pink like a rose
In a swamp, he refuges
Bitter stench, cover your nose.

Bella Weaver (10)
Glebelands Primary Academy, Chatteris

Mysterious Scarers

Sullivan
Ferocious, spotty
Thumping, alarming, stomping
Blue and violet all over
Scare creator
Jittery, waddling, bouncing
One-eyed, bogey-green
Mike.

Dylan Seymour (11)
Glebelands Primary Academy, Chatteris

Monster Poem

Grinch
Green, disrespectful
Cruel, creepy, lies low
Steals Christmas, destroys dreams
Brandishing, catastrophic, ruffled
Hairy stealer, menacing
Monster.

Ruby Grace Gardner (10)
Glebelands Primary Academy, Chatteris

The Blue And Purple Scarer

There was once a monster of purple and blue
Who was waiting in the pongy spray queue
He bought soap of skunk
And smelled like a punk
With some dung caught on his shoe.

Alex Allen (10)
Glebelands Primary Academy, Chatteris

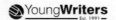

Monstrous Poem
Haiku poetry

Tentacle covered
Cloud-grey coloured, monstrous beast
Chatting lies ahead

Very vibrant hood
A venom-spitting nightmare
Blinding up your street.

Spencer Thompson (10)
Glebelands Primary Academy, Chatteris

Sully

Sully
King scarer
Thundering, creeping, menacing
Scare the children, pounce and roar
Destructive, brandishing, rampaging
Colossal beast
Monster.

Caitlin Lenton (10)
Glebelands Primary Academy, Chatteris

The Grinch
Haiku poetry

It lurks in his cave
Ready to strike his victim
Christmas is ruined

A green dream crusher
Watch out for this destroyer
Slyly thieving gifts.

Kyle Carter (10)
Glebelands Primary Academy, Chatteris

The Green Ogre Who Likes Having A Mud Bath

A green moody monster
Who likes to have a mud bath
Lying in his bed
Waiting until it's midnight
Halloween will be over soon.

Alise Kalva (10)
Glebelands Primary Academy, Chatteris

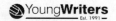

Fluffy The Three-Headed Dog

Fluffy
Three-headed dog
Hiding an unknown jewel
You'd better beware of this beast
Fluffy.

Caitlyn Smith (10)
Glebelands Primary Academy, Chatteris

Grendel

Starving
Murderous, sleek
Slaying, hunting, scoffing
Petrifying everyone to death
Grendel.

Jessica-Leigh Sessions (11)
Glebelands Primary Academy, Chatteris

The Creature In The School Pool

When I was sleeping soundly in my bed
I remembered what my friends had said
That on the scariest, darkest of nights
A creature leaps out and gives you a fright

They say it lurks in the old swimming pool
Covered and drenched in spit, ready to drool
You can hear the dropping of a dime
That sends a trickle of fear up your spine
So I went to investigate in the early morn
And what did I see?
Well, a pile of shoes, damp and torn

That's when I heard it, climbing up the wall
It smelt full of chlorine straight from the pool
It had wet, bumpy skin that looked gruesome and vile
Like something so similar to the stench of mouse bile
But then, just then, gave me a sweet, innocent smile

I screamed, then backed away in fright
It smiled at me again, this time I danced with delight
It was a fuzzy furball, cute and hairy
I don't know why my classmates thought he was scary
At first, he was creepy and so I was wary
That's why I thought that he was so scary

Yes, at first, it gave me a fright
But it could literally run at the speed of light
Zip and zam and zoom again
Would this monster be my friend?
But all of a sudden, it growled at me
Whilst it sat up in a puddle of pee
It gave me a scare
To see something so rare

It stood up, eyes everywhere
As it grew sharp spikes in its long, matted hair
Then it grew eyes, one then two
Until I lost count, but it was more than a few
Then it started to roar and roar and roar
Until it grew so big, I could see it no more

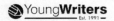

Its eyes were like pools of a raging fire
It had dark blue skin and nails sharp as wire

It reached its hand down for me
But I stood my ground and didn't flee
Just then, my teacher burst into the room
A mad look on her face and her hand on a broom
An epic battle had begun
Between a fluffy Martian and a teacher that's a nun
One of them was about to meet their doom
The Martian won, the teacher knocked out
With a spoon.

Lacey Isobelle Klima (10)
Malvern St James Girls' School, Malvern

It's Hair Not Home

Monsters, monsters everywhere
They're even nesting in your hair
"What shall we do?" everyone cries
They might crawl down and nibble our eyes
They are very fat with eight slimy hands
Four stretchy legs like elastic bands
With a small, tidy beard
And fangs that should be feared
They creep and crawl around your head
And suck your blood while you sleep in bed
"Please make them leave!" I beg my mum
"They might start eating my peachy bum!"
"Oh, don't be silly, you drama queen,
They're only nits, they're not so mean
I know exactly what to do
We'll get the comb and the special shampoo
Those monsters will go from millions to zero!"
My mum is a monster-beating hero!

Isla Wall (10)
Malvern St James Girls' School, Malvern

The Midnight Monster

The old floorboard on the very top stair
Made a creak, it sure gave me a scare
I woke up with a jolt
And sat up like a bolt
I opened the door
And this is what I saw

A pair of eyes as green as grass
A set of teeth, shining like brass
His hand stretched towards me, a greeny-grey
I was scared, so I ran away
I took a breath in and let it out
I tried to scream, no sound came out

I was drenched in cold sweat
I was prepared to bet
That the monster would be back
When I heard a crack
I crept along and looked through the keyhole
And I saw the monster staring into my soul

My fear was going crazy
My terror stopped me being lazy
I lay down and closed my eyes
Please be a dream, my mind vies
I drifted into an uneasy sleep
But I really couldn't resist a peep

I got to the door and opened it wide
And then he ran away to hide
I actually rather miss him
He didn't rip me limb from limb
"Oh please come back!" I said out loud
And then I thought I heard a crowd

There were monsters of every size and shape
My favourite one wore a red cape
My monstrous, laughing friend
He drove me around the bend
Really, it was midnight time
My pranking partner in crime

Now I see him for what he truly is
A triangular guy with some cute fizz
He has short, fat arms and legs
And three-fingered hands, he really begs
For piles and piles of sweet, yummy lobster
In the fridge, my midnight monster.

Izzy Lewis (11)
Malvern St James Girls' School, Malvern

The Wrath Of Lightning Leo

Lightning Leo is an electric eel
He likes children, they're his favourite meal
He's as quiet as a mouse
He can jump as high as a house
Lightning Leo is really real
How do I know?
I know because I am Lightning Leo
And I'm coming to get you
So scream all you want
Lightning Leo is little old me

His bumpy back moves side to side
His scaly skin is like a slide
His inky black eye turns you to stone
His murky scales are like a cone
He lives by himself all alone
He sends electrical shocks down your spine
You will always work for him down the mine
He likes taunting
Especially haunting.

Tilly Coughtrie (9)
Malvern St James Girls' School, Malvern

Shock Fluff

Shock Fluff is a cute fluffball
Who has sharp claws on every paw
And a blue, dotted back
With hands that like to smack.

People who get in his way
Will never see the light of day.
His favourite food is a snot-like pickle,
He has a tail that likes to wiggle.

He comes from far, far south,
Don't go too close or you'll say hello to his mouth.
He will eat you up in one big gulp,
Be aware, don't start to yelp.

Don't touch him, no, no, no.
Be aware, he will grow
Big, fat and very chubby,
He turns into no cute puppy.

He grows warts on his face
Soon there will be no space
For you, me and everyone,
He'll start to weigh a ton.

He will spit
And he may even sit
Upon your head which will hurt very much.
He will squash you unless you are Dutch.

Carry a pole
So you can shoot him into a hole
He will shoot off like a rocket
Remember to put gunpowder in his pocket.

So you will never see him again
Because he will be blasted off to Spain.
Half-crumbled
In the air, he starts to tumble.

When he lands
There will be an explosion in the sand.
People will come from far and wide
To take a selfie by his side.

He will be locked up in a cage
And will be on every newspaper page.
They will pay millions to see him
Be aware, he might stab you with a pin.

When he dies
There will be many cries.
He will turn very dry
So you can eat him in your pie!

Emily Lymer (10)
Malvern St James Girls' School, Malvern

Flap The Monster

Flap has wings that sing
She is small
And she can crawl
The next day
She went to play
That night, she couldn't sleep
Because something was tickling her feet
She took one look at her foot
And there was her big monster friend called Soot
Soot was cuddled up in Flap's bed
Soot said, "My bed is full of lead."
Flap's bed was already full
There wasn't room for a monster as big as a bull
Flap shouted, "There's no room!"
Soot said, "You let me stay here or I'll bring you to your doom!"
Flap said, "Fine, you can stay here!"
But please can you stay near?"

Grace Price (9)
Malvern St James Girls' School, Malvern

Big, Fat, Friendly Brian

Big, fat Brian is a friendly guy
Who really is very shy
Don't scare him or he'll get angry
And it will get very dangly
Because he likes to hang from the ceiling
Everything will start peeling
Nothing will be healing
For this evening
He's calmed down just for now
Be ready for a pounce
It will make you bounce
You will run away
And you will stay
In the place all day

Big, fat Brian is very hungry
If he doesn't eat, he gets very mumbly
And starts to eat anything
And many things get eaten
He starts to spurt out green, thick goo
From it, he shouts, "Boo!"

Holly Forsyth (9)
Malvern St James Girls' School, Malvern

Freaky Fredrick

Freaky Frederick is his name
He creeps and wiggles along your water drain
When you sit on the loo
You wonder where he could be
You realise he's beneath you
He has a slimy tail as thin as can be
Watery eyes that make you need a wee
He has green scales
That shimmer in the day

He may appear in your room
Don't scream or he may get you
The sharp teeth belong to him
They're yellow and green from the swim
He comes far, far south
Always run north
Or you may appear
In his mouth
He lives in a cabin
It's not far
Never go to visit
Or you may come out with a scar.

Emily Aris (10)
Malvern St James Girls' School, Malvern

Cat Claw

Cat Claw has four paws
That scratch through doors
You're never safe when he's in your house
You have to be as quiet as a mouse
If he comes into your room
You will meet your doom
His teeth are razor-sharp
His voice is like a harp
He draws you in close
And then it gets gross
He rips off your limbs
And stands there and grins
As you scream in pain
The more strength he gains
He scoops up your insides
With his pitch-black eyes
His fur dark and dirty brown
And he constantly wears a frown
Cat Claw is a scary cat
Make sure you don't give him a pat.

Jasmine Garner (9)
Malvern St James Girls' School, Malvern

Pickled Trump

There's a rumour going around the school
There's a monster in the pool
With chicken feet and puss-filled spots
His favourite food is grown-ups
The teachers were shocked to hear these things
"What do you mean, child? He doesn't want to eat me!"
Time the cannons and the guns
It was a warzone at the front
They found out it was Trump, they said,
"Golly gosh! It's Donald Trump!
Wow, you're a chunky fella!"
One squeak popped out of his bottom
"I guess that is why they call you Trump!
So what's the Donald for then?"

Sophia Mepsted (10)
Malvern St James Girls' School, Malvern

Wrinklespot

There is a monster who turns into a slug
Who's hairy and scary
And eats lots of bugs

The monster is terrifying
Every time I look in the mirror
It is there

When I put make-up on for special occasions
The slug is still there
Why has it haunted me all my life?
Stop! Please, stop!

But one day, when I went to a party with my make-up on
I heard a scream and a cry
Then I realised the hairy, scary monster
Was nothing more than me
So, every day, the children say
"Oh, Mummy! Please make it go away!"

Fenella Mason (11)
Malvern St James Girls' School, Malvern

Was It Real?

I woke up this morning to a really big fright
I looked in the mirror and saw quite a sight
I saw myself with spots and dots
They looked really big, but they started to rot
Is this karma striking me?
It hurt like the sting of a bee
I needed to go back to bed before I fainted
My blood looked like dark blue and painted
I felt sick, I couldn't get up now
I just really couldn't see how
I fell asleep and did dream and dream
Dream about a pile of cream
Argh! I woke up, what's the deal?
I can't believe this was real!

Charlotte Lorraine Gannon (11)
Malvern St James Girls' School, Malvern

Glad's Life

Glad is a fluffy, cute and horny monster
He is fluffier than a piece of candyfloss
Cuter than a hamster
The horns are like a ram's
It lives under the bed, making happy, golden dreams
While the children sleep so soundly
As small as a cat
He likes hot chocolate
In the dead of night, he will sneak a lot of hot chocolate
He will also sneak a bit of your cucumber
When he has finished making dreams
He will go and have a dip in the relaxing, shining pool
Then he will start to disappear
He is not allowed to be seen at night!

Eleanor Jayne Bradford (9)
Malvern St James Girls' School, Malvern

The Hairy Monster

I'm going to jump in the pool
But then I hear something, it sounds like a tool
I go in the shed and then I see
A hairy monster staring at me
He jumps onto my face and then I cry
"There's a monster poking my eye!"
But then I have a cunning plan
But first, I need to get a tan
After a while, I get some meat
The monster runs off with it and into a cage of wheat
But suddenly, he bites through and jumps into the pool
But now, he looks very cool.

Farah Aftab (9)
Malvern St James Girls' School, Malvern

The Wiggle Giggle Monster

The monster is cute
And does a lot of poop
He likes to giggle
And wiggle
He says, "Hi,"
And starts to cry
He has a lot of fur
And likes to purr
He likes jelly
In his belly
He goes to the park
And likes to bark
He won't be polite
He'll give you a fright
If he jumps up
He will say, "Yum!"
He will rub his tum
And will gobble you up
And say, "That's enough!"

Saba Saghir (9)
Malvern St James Girls' School, Malvern

The Cat Paw!

There is a rumour going around
Of a monster that makes no sound

He is really fluffy and has long claws
His teeth are sharp, just like a bear's

He has small wings to fly about
And has tiny arms and a pig-like snout

I don't think this story is true
But my friends have seen him in the loo

Being mean and spreading goo
Last night, I saw his open jaws

He waved to me with his fluffy cat paws.

Lauren Iris Jolley (9)
Malvern St James Girls' School, Malvern

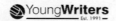

Pickleta The #1 Beast

I am Pickleta, I am wonderful and green
I am tall and lean
I am proud
I'm also very loud
I've got a big bow
That I like to show

I'm a bad beast
That likes a good feast
I like Monster Munch
For lunch
I like noses
And toes

I spread pickle juice
And I like to let loose
I kill children with my spell
So I send them to Hell
My eyes attack
But they're just to distract.

Sophia Michael (10)
Malvern St James Girls' School, Malvern

Sugar Sweet

Sugar Sweet
Was walking in the street
It was a sunny day
When she went to play
She went to the park
And saw a dog bark
She was so scared
And the mean dog just glared
Sugar ran away
But the dog just wanted to play
The dog chased after Sugar Sweet
And ran down the street
Sugar Sweet was out of breath
And she was so scared to death
She stopped to breathe the air
And saw a ball of hair behind her.

Carlota de Palacio (9)
Malvern St James Girls' School, Malvern

Little Poppy Pou

There is a little monster that I know
And he loves to play in snow
He is very cute and very fluffy
He is even nicer than Miss Duffy
This monster loves to jump around
Then fall onto the solemn ground

Crash! Boom! Bam! Bash!
Metal pots and metal hats
Crash! Boom! Bam! Bash!
He had a sugar rush and had a hash

And, by the way, if you didn't know
His name is little Poppy Pou.

Beulah Naami Emmanuel (10)
Malvern St James Girls' School, Malvern

Colossal Cow

Here comes Colossal Cow
She's the hero of the town
She's brave and fierce
She'll solve your fears
She squeezes poison milk from her udder
And all the baddies shake and shudder
Her rocket boots allow her to fly
And the suction cups allow her to climb up high
She goes to the moovies with her friends
And hugs them all until the film ends.

Tilly Delamore (10)
Malvern St James Girls' School, Malvern

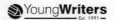

The Head-Gobbler

Everyone is terrified
About the monster outside
He strikes fear into anyone's eyes
He scoffs gargantuan, grubby flies
He climbs up walls
You can't hear his calls
He is quieter than a mouse
So close the windows in your house
Or he might creep and crawl
Along your upstairs hall
And sneak into your bed
To gobble up your head.

Alice Kay-Jones (10)
Malvern St James Girls' School, Malvern

Terrifying Tanka

Torturing people,
At midnight sneaking around,
Tearing up the ground,
Always staring at people,
Disguised whenever he wants.

Like a chameleon, being scared when people walk past.

Huge, humongous spikes,
Pulverising everything,
Hiding day and night,
Knowing where his prey's hidden,
Crushing every little bone.

Like a full-grown menacing hyena.

Killing whenever,
Tearing up what he can eat,
Munching every day,
It is roaming, repugnant,
He is daring, devilish.

Like a lion, pouncing at its prey.

Sam Anderson (10)
Riccall Community Primary School, Riccall

Party The Party Monster

One multicoloured, shiny party hat,
Gleaming, glistening, sparkling, glowing.

Two blue, bulging eyes,
Looking, blinking, opening, closing.

Three white, gargantuan teeth,
Chomping, chewing, eating, swallowing.

Four green, pointy arms,
Pointing, cheering, waving, moving.

Five pink, smirky mouths,
Smiling, grinning, eating, chomping.

Four red, elf-like shoes,
Walking, running, jogging, jumping.

Three black, pig-like snouts,
Sniffling, breathing, wiggling, dripping.

Two brown, cat-like ears,
Hearing, twitching, flapping, glistening.

One orange, stubby leg,
Hopping, falling, walking, running.

Jemma Johnson (10)
Riccall Community Primary School, Riccall

Robot Spook

R obot
O ut in your room
B eware if he tears you
O ver and under you as you're asleep
T error

One scarlet, gargantuan mouth,
Gnashing, ripping, demolishing, devouring,
Four emerald, diamond eyes,
Studying, blinking, rolling, staring,
Fifteen yellow, sharp teeth,
Waiting, chomping, eating, swallowing,
Two red, round noses,
Sniffing, smelling, breathing, inhaling.

S cary
P rowling around
O ut at the murder scene
O ut watching you sleep in your bed
K illing!

Nicola Louise Rodwell (11)
Riccall Community Primary School, Riccall

The Monsters

Watch out!
For the monster,
Stalking from under your bed,
Listening, smelling, tasting, feeling,
Watch out!

- **M** onsters are everywhere,
- **O** ozing acid from their eyes,
- **N** aughty monsters eating children,
- **S** melling, scary, snake-like creature,
- **T** earing hands, grabbing,
- **E** ating little children,
- **R** oaring like a dinosaur,
- **S** tealing some snacks and children to eat.

Watch out!
He is out here now!
To eat every child...
Devouring children's bones.
Watch out!

Harry Blake (10)
Riccall Community Primary School, Riccall

The Malicious, Malignant Monster

Six blood-red, listening ears,
Drooping, dangling,
Paying attention to you, like a dog waiting for its owner,
Hanging, melting.

Four blue, glaring eyes,
Twitching, glowing,
Watching me like a hawk stalking its prey,
Blinking, staring.

Six gold, munching teeth,
Demolishing, destroying,
Drooling like a lion when it sees its food,
Crunching, gobbling.

Nine green, clawing fingers,
Scratching, clutching,
Nails as long as wolves' claws, scratching at people,
Gnashing, tearing.

Ellie Chambers (10)
Riccall Community Primary School, Riccall

Terminator

Two red, glaring eyes,
Staring, watching, waiting, glaring.

Two long, hairy legs stomping,
Like an earthquake breaking up the ground.

Two huge, round eyes glaring,
Like an eagle stalking its prey.

Two huge, muscly arms strangling little children,
Like a gorilla killing its prey.

A million little teeth,
Munching, crunching, smiling, shining.

This monster's name is the Terminator,
And he is the most horrifying beast you will ever see!

Oscar Squires (10)
Riccall Community Primary School, Riccall

Gloopy Green Goggleamore

Crawling towards me
(Like a snake in a forest)
Is a blob of slime.

Two bright blue, balloon-like eyes,
Penetrating, hypnotising, staring into your soul,
Two black bat wings,
Flapping, thrashing, beating in the air,
Six slimy, stretching arms,
Wriggling, wobbling, wrapping around you,
Five foul teeth, feasting like a shark,
Gnashing, mashing, attempting to eat you.

His mouth opens wide,
He's malicious and slimy,
I'm lost inside him.

Finley Woodroffe (10)
Riccall Community Primary School, Riccall

Monsters

Spreads from house to house,
Spiteful and solitary,
Seeps inside your mind.

Three scrutinising eyes,
Observing their victims like a hawk,
One formidable, flaming body,
Like an active volcano, about to explode,
Two revolving, ebony antennae,
Rotating like a helicopter's propellers,
One despicable personality,
Malevolent, like a tiger pouncing on its prey.

Vexed and venomous,
Malicious and malignant,
Be very afraid!

Sophia Astrid Robinson (10)
Riccall Community Primary School, Riccall

Horror Haikus

It likes to eat kids,
With his sharp, yellow, long teeth,
Like a hungry shark.

It roams through the streets,
Waiting, listening, feasting,
Run or it will come.

Its hideous face,
It looks like a three-eyed troll,
Coming to eat you.

It's coming for you,
Drooling like a hungry dog,
Watch out! It's coming.

As fast as a car,
With his four super-fast legs,
Charging down your street.

Toby Alexander Steward (10)
Riccall Community Primary School, Riccall

Terrifying Tankas

Monster: it's coming,
With metal spike balls as hands,
Monster: it's closer,
With one tail trailing behind,
Monster: it's entering now!

The sound of its feet
Stomping on the stony floor.
Its skin dragging down
Slimy scales separating,
Exposing its strong muscles.

It has me cornered,
Destroying everybody,
Will it destroy me?
It gets closer and closer,
Then opens its drooling jaws!

Jack Duffy (10)
Riccall Community Primary School, Riccall

The Malevolent Monster (Tankas)

I see a shadow,
An eerie, gloomy shadow.
I hear loud wwwhiirrinng,
Constant, high whirring noises,
Like a machine in a lab.

I notice a stench,
An evil and rotten stench.
I feel a shiver,
A constant, crawling shiver,
Like a spider up my spine.

I need to look now.
What is lurking around there?
The tension builds up.
It looks like, no it can't be...
A malevolent monster!

Charlie Anderson (10)
Riccall Community Primary School, Riccall

This Monster

This monster eats a lot of food
He is as grey as concrete,
Every day he goes out, trying to find some friends,
He is as big as King Kong.

He is mean at night,
He is never nice at night,
His breath never smells.

Whenever he is going to bed, he always brushes his teeth,
His eyes are as shiny as a mirror,
He always reads books in his bedroom,
His hair is as fluffy as a cat.

Lewis Porteous (10)
Riccall Community Primary School, Riccall

Monster Acrostic

M unching on children,
O n a rampage through the street,
N ever go near him, he will attack,
S it and pray if he ever comes,
T reats (to him) are the bigger children - he eats them in one big gulp,
E veryone knows that he is the worst,
R espect him and leave him alone, or you will die,
S o now you've been warned: don't go out at night.

Kadie Olivia Kettlewell (10)
Riccall Community Primary School, Riccall

The Exterminator

Devouring children
Exterminating humans
Petrifying all
Stabbing people every day
Torturing humans proudly.

The evil creature
A monstrous, mean maniac
A huge, heartless beast
Slashing people to pieces
The evil, mega-sized beast.

The ultra killer
He is a true predator
Killing everything
Destroying the human race
The true king of the monsters.

Ashton Clayton (10)
Riccall Community Primary School, Riccall

The Chaotic Cat

Four violent, gargantuan tails,
Swiping, swooshing, swishing, sliding.

Two green, chunky arms,
Flapping, whipping, flexing, sweating.

Two yellow, spotty ears,
Twitching, pointing, stretching, listening.

Two white, mysterious eyes,
Wiggling, winking, watching, waiting.

Two pink, tusk-like teeth,
Demolishing, devouring, smashing, gnashing.

Katie Rose Hardwick (10)
Riccall Community Primary School, Riccall

The Mechanical Ghost

Two red, googly eyes,
Bobbing, winking, wobbling, bobbling.

Two fox-like ears,
Twitching, wriggling, shape-shifting, swishing.

One red, red, wiggling tongue,
Licking, slobbering, flopping, slopping.

Two grey ghostly mechanical arms,
Grabbing, throwing, crushing, mushing.

One white ghostly body,
Floating, flying, scary, hairy.

Billy Hitrof Swan (11)
Riccall Community Primary School, Riccall

The Monster

Monster,
Looking for food,
Lurking in the dark woods,
Eating its prey, blood dripping down,
Monster.

Two yellow, glowing eyes,
Looking, staring, blinking, rolling,
Two red arms, grabbing,
Wiggling, wobbling, muscling, clutching.

Monster,
Terrifying,
Walking back to its den,
Waiting for night to fall again,
To hunt.

Cameron Roche (10)
Riccall Community Primary School, Riccall

My Monster

Cute, cuddly, chaotic,
Like a new puppy jumping on the sofa,
Mischievous, meddling monster,
Like a party popper ready to explode in the living room,
Triangular tuft of tickles,
Like a feathered finger,
Hectic, hazardous hands,
Like a mess-machine ready to cause chaos,
Flurrying fast feet,
Like a greyhound, speeding to the finish line.

Laura-Rose Arkless McKie (11)
Riccall Community Primary School, Riccall

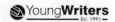

Bluesill The Lonely

Bluesill,
Miserable,
Perishing in the snow,
Isolated from the others,
Depressed.

Bulky,
Big, blue bowtie,
As cold as an ice block,
Horns as thick as a metal wall,
Friendless.

Gentle,
Large, turquoise eyes,
As sweet as marshmallows,
A misunderstood little soul,
Lonely.

Ruby Baron (10)
Riccall Community Primary School, Riccall

The Mean Monster

M y monster envelopes children like an,
O mnivore engulfing its food,
N ibbling, gnawing, enveloping, gnashing,
S cratching, slicing and slashing at children,
T errible panther pouncing on its prey,
E xterminating, killing, assassinating,
R emember to be in fear of the beast.

Sam Quormby Gowland (10)
Riccall Community Primary School, Riccall

Two Terrifying Tankas!

Stripy legs like socks,
Tearing and gnashing children,
Horns, sharp as daggers,
His diamond glows like the sun,
Glaring at you in your sleep.

His nails are snake teeth,
Roaming houses in moonlight,
Crunching everyone,
Sharp teeth grinding you at night,
His body smashes countries.

Abigail Ayre (10)
Riccall Community Primary School, Riccall

The Scary Thing Cinquain

S omething
C oming closer
A lways around, hiding
R eally, he is protective of...
Y es, me!

T witching
H ow's he so still?
I 'm so glad he's doing so
N o one knows my furry thing's there
G ood thing!

Millie Bradley (10)
Riccall Community Primary School, Riccall

The Sludge Monster

One red, creepy eye,
Staring, looking, following, moving.

Two white, needle-point fangs,
Gnashing, chomping, chewing, intimidating.

Two green, oozing arms,
Grabbing, clutching, glooping, sludging.

Two red, pointy horns,
Stabbing, demolishing, charging, tearing.

Dziugas Gelbuda (11)
Riccall Community Primary School, Riccall

The Horrifying Haikus

A terrifying
Monster, spiteful, malicious
Petrifying kids.

A gargantuan
Monster, colossal, massive
Stomping on adults.

A nauseating
Monster, repulsive and gross
Consuming people.

A skinny, bony
Monster, starving, ravenous
Trying to eat me.

Max Butterfield (10)
Riccall Community Primary School, Riccall

Horrifying Tankas

Tearing up the ground,
Pulverising little kids,
Nauseating legs,
Scaring the life from people,
Knowing where his prey's hidden.

Hiding in the woods,
Creating disgusting webs,
Demolishing things,
Readying to pounce at you,
Scaring people day and night.

Jake Wilman (10)
Riccall Community Primary School, Riccall

Fierce Fluffy

M y monster is as fluffy as a feather,
O nly my monster has a tooth as white as a freshly painted wall,
N ever naughty, never a nuisance,
S potty like a ladybug,
T icklish toes and a tiny top hat,
E gg-shaped body,
R eally responsible.

Georgia Saunders (10)
Riccall Community Primary School, Riccall

The Monster

Two black, bold eyes,
Staring, glaring, darting, popping.

Four yellow, mouldy teeth,
Shredding, gnashing, tearing, scraping.

Two green, microscopic arms,
Stubby, miniature, tiny, twisted.

One pink, slimy tongue,
Slurping, prolonged, gritty, gruesome.

Madison Main (11)
Riccall Community Primary School, Riccall

The Terrifying Tanka

Floating over me,
Mischievous, menacing, mean,
Terrifying me,
Hovering over my bed,
Turning my light on and off.

Flying next to me,
Frightening, fearsome, fiendish,
Petrifying me,
When dad comes and checks on me,
He becomes a lamp or chair.

Josh Light (11)
Riccall Community Primary School, Riccall

Horrible Haikus

This is a monster
And he will devour you
He eats anything.

Loves ripping bodies
Terrible teeth tear apart
All things in their way.

He is so greedy
He would love to eat you too
Look! Run! He's coming!

Oliver Capewell (11)
Riccall Community Primary School, Riccall

Terrifying

Spiteful
Do you believe
In the tattle-tale rock
The computer virus
Do you?

Magic
That's what you need
The great unknown wants you
Be afraid, it's coming for you
It's here.

Roma Sofia Gatenby (10)
Riccall Community Primary School, Riccall

Petrifying Haiku

Tarnished teeth tearing,
Ghostly, gory, grisly, green,
Pointy, haunted nose.

Arms flexing around,
Big, bulky, bulging biceps,
Ready to attack.

Luke Sparham (10)
Riccall Community Primary School, Riccall

The Hairy Spike

Beware of Hairy Spike!
He hides under your bed,
And if your feet hang out,
He will chop them off, so say bye-bye.

If you come out at night you might die,
Or get a surprise!
And every Halloween,
It grows his appetite,
You might get a fright,
He will eat your parents,
With his sharp, black teeth.

Beware of Hairy Spike!
But if it is not Halloween or any scary day,
You will be fine,
So if you see one I will tell you what he looks like,
He has sparkly, spiky, sharp spikes,
His hair is soft scruff.

Emily Grace Soulsby (8)
St Benet's RC Primary School, Sunderland

Scary Monsters

Monsters, scary monsters,
Tough monsters, strong,
Maybe you open the door,
And you hear a scary, scary monster,
Monsters, big monsters,
Small monsters,
Short monsters, tall,
Maybe one called Smoky,
Will do okay,
Scary, scary monsters live amongst us,
Scary, scary monsters,
See for yourself,
And find out,
Monsters, scary monsters,
Under your bed,
You hear them cough up cobwebs,
From under your bed,
Scary, scary monsters,
Out at night,
Monsters eat odd stuff,
Like bugs and all that.

Emily Maw (8)
St Benet's RC Primary School, Sunderland

Monster Mash

The wind howls loudly,
And the grass sways wildly,
The thunder bangs strongly,
And the lightning flashes wrongly,
All the monsters come out at night,
So beware because all the children will be scared tonight,
The witches with their brooms,
And the ghosts with their *boos*,
But there is this one monster who is the best of them all,
She's scary, she's hairy and she's very awful,
She's got giant horns and a great big mouth,
And she's called Naughty Nia,
So beware because you will be very scared.

Scarlett Shickle (8)
St Benet's RC Primary School, Sunderland

Delightful Spike

Delightful, dirty, disgraceful Spike,
He had a best friend called Perfect Pike,
Pike had trouble building his nest,
He wanted to enter a competition and be the best,
Perfect Pike always gets covered with leaves,
Spike's help he may receive,
All the big owls did was take the twigs,
Over behind the trees, there was a shop filled with wigs,
Spike came along to help Pike,
They finished the nest, just Pike and Spike,
Pike's nest was great and certainly not lame,
Pike won and is now in the hall of fame.

Ella Clasper (8)
St Benet's RC Primary School, Sunderland

Monsters

Monsters, monsters, big
And wide but sometimes,
They don't always like pie,
Oh, weird and funny monsters.

The monsters, monsters,
That are big and hairy,
But sometimes they remind me
Of Hairy McLairy.

Mother, Mother,
There's a monster under
My bed, wait a minute,
I think I will call him Fred.

Monsters, monsters,
On the floor, wait,
How is it as big as a door?
Who is afraid of monsters?

Damaris Osigwelem (9)
St Benet's RC Primary School, Sunderland

The Monster Under My Bed

Every night before I go to sleep, me and my teddy, Mr Ted,
Think there's a monster underneath my bed.
One night he came out, his teddy was blue,
The strange creature was about four feet, actually, add on another two.
I think the monster will be mean,
Because he ate my last jellybean!
The monster told me his name is Kyle,
And surprisingly he can run one mile.
When he's tired he starts to moan,
And when I get bored, I start to groan.

Evie Selkirk (8)
St Benet's RC Primary School, Sunderland

Bedtime Monsters

Monsters wait for children to sleep,
They don't make a screech,
In the night, the children have a light,
So they can sleep tight,
The light keeps them from getting a fright of the
Bedtime Monsters,
If you have your light off,
The monsters might get you,
So hide under the covers before they get you,
You might have a poo!
Try not to make a peep,
Just have a light,
So you won't get a fright of the,
Bedtime Monsters.

Scarlett Dawn Glendenning (8)
St Benet's RC Primary School, Sunderland

Cheeky Monsters

When all the children are asleep,
Out come the monsters as they peep,
They come out at night,
They break your toys,
They're scary and hairy, they're not nice,
They steal things without paying the price,
And the only thing they eat is ice,
They have really loud yawns,
But they don't mow your lawn,
They break and shake your toys,
They kill bears,
And pull your hair,
And do it because they don't care.

Eva Wilkinson (8)
St Benet's RC Primary School, Sunderland

Mr Mugly Poem

Every night, when I'm asleep,
The monster group crawls into my room,
One stays, the others go,
Mugly is the one alone,
He says to me,
"It doesn't matter if you are short or tall,"
Because Mugly loves us all,
If you're grumpy, happy, mad or all,
It doesn't matter because Mugly
Always gives you your all,
Mugly, Mugly,
Where are you?
Boo!
I'm snuggling with you.

Izzy Rose Balcombe (8)
St Benet's RC Primary School, Sunderland

Little Monster

Down the stairs and in a room, lies a monster,
Just like you,
Through the bathroom and through the yard,
Howling noises coming soon,
People running through the school,
As I meet you eating food,
Should I stay, or should I not?
Thinking just as I look,
Oh no, it's you, you're brown,
You're cute and loud,
He is now back in his room, sleeping fast,
What's he thinking,
Your chance to think.

Katie Ward (8)
St Benet's RC Primary School, Sunderland

Demon's Haunted Race

Oh no! I've lost my place in the race,
I wish I was a fast mouse,
Then I would win the haunted house.

I am going to take that shortcut,
I just wish I didn't have to do it with my own foot.

Yes, now I am going to win,
Oh no, here's a massive bin,
That has just hurt me,
I think I've got a broken knee.

Okay, I have got back on track.
Oh, I wish I took a path.

Poppy Robson (8)
St Benet's RC Primary School, Sunderland

The Halloween Skeleton

A spooky, scary skeleton shivers down your spine,
It sees your doors and wakes your dorms,
You won't believe your sight,
When you see him it's a fright,
It's scarier than your dreams at night,
His bones clatter everywhere, making a racket,
He comes out on Halloween, he probably takes your snacks,
However, every night he always eats too much,
He's coming for you, run away, watch out!

Hannah Elizabeth Banks (8) & Emilia Szewczyk
St Benet's RC Primary School, Sunderland

The Monster Under My Bed

There's a monster called Demon under my bed,
She's red and fluffy,
But not very friendly,
She bites and gives me a fright,
My mum and dad just don't believe me,
Now I'm getting quite weary,
She chews up my teddies,
Which is quite mean,
Because I hate to clean,
She ate my last jelly bean,
Now I have to go to bed,
With Ned,
My teddy,
Who has no head.

Ruby Laidler-Gilchrist (8)
St Benet's RC Primary School, Sunderland

The Misunderstood Monster

I was walking home from school that night,
Then something caught my sight,
So I came closer and it was big and black,
It collected children in its sack,
And it loved to whack,
Also, grab people on the back,
It hid in the black,
How frightening it is, there is nothing he lacks,
He eats children as snacks,
And he also loves to eat cats.

Archie McGuire (8)
St Benet's RC Primary School, Sunderland

Scary Monster

Scary, scary monster,
There's one in the closet,
Scary, scary monster,
On the sofa,
Scary, scary monster,
Playing on the Xbox,
Scary, scary monster,
Sleeping in my bed,
Scary, scary monster,
Making a big shriek,
Scary, scary monster,
Even on the toilet,
There's one, all gone,
Because of my mummy!

Daniel Hewitt (9)
St Benet's RC Primary School, Sunderland

Spooky Scary Spotty The Snore Monster

Spooky Scary Spotty sends shivers down your spine,
As he stomps through the night,
He will step on you,
And stomp on you,
So don't move or you'll end up under his big feet,
So be careful!
Or he'll be after you,
So I will say it again,
Don't move and just go to sleep!
Please!

Maddie Harrison (8)
St Benet's RC Primary School, Sunderland

Fancy Fang At Night

Look under your bed,
You might find something fluffy or spiky,
So be careful!
Otherwise you might get a fright,
So watch out,
Because the monsters are out tonight,
Stay under your covers,
In case the monster takes you between his jaws,
Hear the door creak,
Then don't make a peep.

Alice Wright (8)
St Benet's RC Primary School, Sunderland

Scary, Spooky Skeleton

Scary, spooky skeleton,
Reaching down your spine,
If you feel a tickle,
You better check your spine,
Scary, spooky skeleton,
Lived in the nearby skip tip,
As the scary, spooky had nowhere to live,
He ate everything he could,
And if you see him in the nearby tip,
Go, go, go!

Peter Rogers (8)
St Benet's RC Primary School, Sunderland

My Friendly Monster

Your teeth are like thorns,
Your hair is spiky,
If you ever see a monster,
Get ready for a fright,
Because they only come out on Halloween night,
They'll steal all of your sweets,
They'll creep around your house,
But the thing is, they are as quiet as a mouse.

Aiesha Potts (9)
St Benet's RC Primary School, Sunderland

The Haunted Dummy

Hello, hello,
Fellow friend,
I am the dummy, who could be coming for you,
I am the person, who could be your nightmare,
I wear an all-black suit that is as dark as the night sky,
I am as creepy as a clown,
So you better watch out, I could be coming for you!

Isaac Fowler (8)
St Benet's RC Primary School, Sunderland

Scary Fellow

Hello, hello, fellow, fellow,
I don't know how I got here,
But I am facing my worst fear,
I saw a ghost and it was a he,
But it could have been a she,
I think the ghost was toast,
It was its sharp teeth that scared me most!

Gabriel Cleugh (9)
St Benet's RC Primary School, Sunderland

The Utterly Weird And Cheeky Monster

Strawberry has very sharp fangs,
Every time she walks, she makes loud bangs,
She is very gentle,
Never that mental,
Strawberry is a bit hairy,
She eats a lot of dairy,
Her red hair,
Is so unfair.

She has black spots,
Always gets lots,
Strawberry is nice,
She has head lice,
She has snake-like arms,
She owns 400 farms,
Strawberry isn't scary,
Like I said, very hairy.

Strawberry is not that fluffy,
But is a little bit puffy,
She is not that short,
But helps at an airport,
Her friends are cool,
She's an absolute fool,
Strawberry is a girl,
She shines like a pearl.

Logan Star Henderson-Thompson (9)
Wheatfield Primary School, Winnersh

Whicker Dog Max

'Twas a Tuesday night on the sixth of October,
1986, a man was tearing a clover,
Suddenly, behind him, he heard a strange noise,
It was a bunch of young teenagers, he shouted,
"You, boys!"
Suddenly the teenagers fled with fear,
The man heard some whispering in his ear,
He turned around, stopped dead in his tracks,
'Twas the legendary Whicker Dog Max!
After the morning, the police came to thrash it,
But the only thing left was a bunch of old ashes,
Whicker Dog Max smashes through the gate,
Whicker Dog Max is not going to be late!

Herbert Whitaker (9)
Wheatfield Primary School, Winnersh

The Naughty George

He's pretty in the city,
But when he's walking down the street, he gets angry and starts to heat,
He's a shorty but a sporty,
Mental but gentle,
He has a long tongue but a fat bum,
He's shooting but hooting,
His body is spotty, his mind is dotty,
He lives near a bog, just like a frog,
He loves to eat flies but hates mince pies,
He's horny and thorny, and silly like Lily,
He's very bold but hates the cold
He loves the warm but prefers a storm,
His eye is as big as a fry.

Lily Scarlett Wears (9)
Wheatfield Primary School, Winnersh

Spot!

Creak, crack,
Mind out for Spot,
Spot has a dot on her head,
She comes out at night,
And parties at day,
In her hideout,
It's called Purple Bearpel,
In Purple Bearpel there's a cauldron,
For her dinner on Friday she has children,
Child dinner,
Next to her cauldron, there's a red bed,
The dot on Spot,
If you look at it for more than five seconds you will drop dead,
Then the cops will come,
At night she will only bite,
At night don't be scared.

Constance Ann Thrift (9)
Wheatfield Primary School, Winnersh

Lorreta The Forgetter

She's pretty in the city,
She's shooting and hooting,
She's mental but gentle,
And puffy and fluffy.

She has a cupcake on her head,
Which she creates in her sugar shed.

Her stars are like cars, they have pretty glass,
Her ribbons sing rhythms when she looks at brass,
She turns soft like astroturf grass,
Her mind is dotty,
Which makes her feel like she needs to be spotty,
She's glittery walking about town,
Acting like she owns a crown.

Ava Rae Henderson-Thompson (9)
Wheatfield Primary School, Winnersh

The Multicoloured Monster

There is a monster called Packietee-tee,
He has a bumblebee,
Packietee-tee has only one friend, called Tangs,
She has bright bangs.

They went out with his bug,
When they got outside they saw the baker, Doug,
Then they saw some doves,
That Tangs loves.

They saw Buzz doing skills with his sword,
They watched Buzz for hours, but then they got bored,
They went back to Tangs' house and played with a box,
After Packietee-tee plaited Tangs' locks.

Evangeline Cozens (10)
Wheatfield Primary School, Winnersh

The Worst Nightmare!

Hooky Tuk-Tuk slithers silently,
Ready to kill you violently,
As quiet as a mouse,
He slithers through the house.

Hooky Tuk-Tuk has fangs,
Bigger than boomerangs,
He would kill you like a dragon would,
And he easily could.

Hooky Tuk-Tuk has a poisonous tail,
And teeth sharper than nails,
Tuk-Tuk can transform himself,
He doesn't need any wealth.

Hooky Tuk-Tuk is ready to strike,
In the dead of night!

Michael Nash (9)
Wheatfield Primary School, Winnersh

The Mosquito Giant

Giant is so angry,
I think he should have a little time-out,
Giant hides under every bed and scares people,
And when he sees a person he eats them,
He is ugly and buggy,
The mosquito bee stings you and pinches people,
Giant is sometimes brave,
Giant is so short, he is one inch,
He likes eating goo,
He is so dumb, he would walk off a cliff,
He lives in a creepy house, the roof fell off,
And he can't go in the city,
He is blue.

Kai Driscoll (9)
Wheatfield Primary School, Winnersh

The Devilish Angel

He hides in the day,
Buries himself in hay,
At night he comes out,
With a scream and a shout.

He'll swallow you whole,
You'll be trapped, like a stuck mole,
He'll crunch on a bone,
Whilst you feel so alone.

So remember at night,
Hide,
Or you might be in for a fright.

He hides in the day,
Buries himself in hay,
At night he comes out,
With a scream and a shout.

Aum Patel (9)
Wheatfield Primary School, Winnersh

Vampire Spiky

Vampire Spiky,
Is very frightening,
He is not likely helpful,
His fangs give bangs when he eats garlic,
He has a gang with Frankenstein,
As Vampire Spiky scares people at night,
He is very scary and he also bites,
He is very hairy and he hates fairies,
Because they don't give him teeth or money,
And he so does not care,
He likes to eat chocolate dairy.

Tailor Cauldwell (9)
Wheatfield Primary School, Winnersh

The Monster

He is fat,
But his nails are as thick as a bat,
And does not like torn hats,
Even squeaky rats,
But likes to sit on comfy mats,
And loves when people say 'congrats',
But hates it when they say he is a brat.

His tummy grumbles,
And he often mumbles,
But never tumbles,
But again, his tummy rumbles,
But he is not humble.

Konstantinos Alkinoos Servos (9)
Wheatfield Primary School, Winnersh

Blobby Wants Candy

I can feel Blobby under my bed,
I can see her head,
She is looking for candy,
But if she doesn't get any,
She will scream loudly,
If she sees a person,
She can shoot her cuteness for candy,
She is really cheeky,
But needy for candy,
She will trick people,
Then lick them,
She learnt how to fly,
When she was only nine!

Alex Cazacu (9)
Wheatfield Primary School, Winnersh

Beware The Coggledog

Beware the Coggledog, with long, brown horns,
And in his mouth sit teeth like thorns,
With tough jaws like metal and a tongue as long as a snake,
Its toenails are as big and as sharp as a rake,
Beware the Coggledog, it comes out at night,
It likes to steal candy and give you a fright,
So beware the Coggledog, it might bite!

Ava Quinn (9)
Wheatfield Primary School, Winnersh

Monstrosity!

Monstrosity is slow,
And his scales always glow,
Monstrosity can fly,
But hates saying goodbye.

Monstrosity lives in a trench,
And he has a golden bench,
He loves breathing fire,
And is an electrifier.

He has enormous wings,
And has lots to bring,
He is a king,
And has a bling ring.

Akhilesh Molala (9)
Wheatfield Primary School, Winnersh

The Crawler

The Crawler is taller than you think
Before you can blink,
He's gone in a *tink*,
He has sticky pads for hands and feet,
But children are a treat,
At night,
Beware of the venomous bite,
It's a deadly fight,
His height is as tall as a male bull,
He never follows.

Vinnie Valentine (9)
Wheatfield Primary School, Winnersh

Pixsie, The Monster At Night

She comes at night,
Just for a bite,
She leaves in the morning,
When you're snoring.

She's fluffy and puffy,
Bad and mad,
She has horns like thorns.

She's mental but gentle,
Sometimes she's nice,
With sugar and spice.

Tiaana Amileah Lee (10)
Wheatfield Primary School, Winnersh

The White Ninja Of Doom!

The white ninja steals stuff,
But money he stuffs,
When the police come,
He is gone...

No one knows where he goes,
But some say he has a foe,
Maybe they were frenemies,
But now enemies.

Abhiram Anumolu (9)
Wheatfield Primary School, Winnersh

YOUNG WRITERS INFORMATION

We hope you have enjoyed reading this book – and that you will continue to in the coming years.

If you're a young writer who enjoys reading and creative writing, or the parent of an enthusiastic poet or story writer, do visit our website www.youngwriters.co.uk. Here you will find free competitions, workshops and games, as well as recommended reads, a poetry glossary and our blog. There's lots to keep budding writers motivated to write!

If you would like to order further copies of this book, or any of our other titles, then please give us a call or order via your online account.

Young Writers
Remus House
Coltsfoot Drive
Peterborough
PE2 9BF
(01733) 890066
info@youngwriters.co.uk

Join in the conversation!
Tips, news, giveaways and much more!

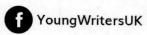 YoungWritersUK

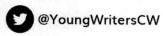 @YoungWritersCW